"Christ said, 'Take heed therefore how ye hear' (Luke 8:18). Brian Najapfour's advice for how to listen to sermons is wise, practical, biblical, and succinct—an excellent guide for how to 'receive with meekness' the Word of God, 'which is able to save your souls' (James 1:21). Every church member would benefit from reading this well-written little book."

—Dr. Joel R. Beeke, President, Puritan Reformed Theological Seminary, Grand Rapids, Michigan

"Most Christians are blessed to hear many sermons through the years of their walk with God. Surely every true believer wants to profit as much as possible from the sermons they hear. If all Christians would apply the principles in this booklet, their spiritual lives would be healthier and our churches would be stronger."

—Dr. Donald S. Whitney, Professor of Biblical Spirituality and Associate Dean at The Southern Baptist Theological Seminary and author of *Spiritual Disciplines for the Christian Life* and *Praying the Bible*

"I was hearing a sermon but missed out on the blessing others later spoke of receiving, and it was because I lacked the ears to hear it. Do not be a hearer only, but by the Spirit listen so as to appropriate what God is saying. This book will assist you much in doing so. He that has ears to hear, let him hear!"

—Rev. Geoff Thomas, former pastor of Alfred Place Baptist Church, Aberystwyth, Wales, for fifty years and author of *The Holy Spirit*

———————————————

"There are many books addressed to preachers (and rightfully so), but there are very few books addressed to those who listen to sermons. This helpful book guides listeners how to be active, intentional, and biblical in their listening to the preached Word of God."

—Rev. Talman Wagenmaker, pastor of Dutton United Reformed Church, Caledonia, Michigan

———————————————

A Hearer of God's Word

A HEARER OF GOD'S WORD

Ten Ways to Listen to Sermons Better

Brian G. Najapfour

Reformed
Fellowship Inc.
www.reformedfellowship.net

A Hearer of God's Word: Ten Ways to Listen to Sermons Better

©2019 by Brian G. Najapfour

Reformed Fellowship, Inc.
(877) 532–8510
president@reformedfellowship.net

Unless otherwise indicated, all Scripture quotations are from The Holy Bible, English Standard Version, copyright © 2001 by Crossway, a publishing ministry of Good News Publishers. Used by permission. All rights reserved.

Book design by Jeff Steenholdt

ISBN 978-1-935369-18-9

To

Trevor Meerdink,

a generous brother in Christ, trusted friend,

and courageous fellow soldier of the Lord

Contents

Preface

This book was born out of the pulpit of my former congregation, Dutton United Reformed Church. On November 19, 2017, I preached a message on how to listen to a sermon. This message was a part of my series on the elements of a public worship service. Many who heard this message encouraged and advised me to consider publishing this sermon. I took their advice; hence, the publication of this book, which is an expanded and edited version of my message. The goal of this book is to help us become better worshipers of God by becoming better sermon listeners. The sermon is the longest element of our worship service. Thus, most of our time in worship is spent listening. Since God expects us to participate in our worship of Him, that means we can't be good worshipers unless we also become good listeners. Listening and worshiping go hand in hand: to listen to God's proclaimed Word is to worship the God of this Word.

I would like to thank Gina Bessetti-Reyes, Josh Dear, Ryan Hurd, and Andrew Buss for their editorial assistance. Without their help, this book may not have been completed. I also wish to thank David Murray for his permission to include his article in this book. This article, entitled "How to Criticize a Preacher," is published here as appendix 2. Of course, gratitude also goes to my dear wife, Sarah, who always supports me whenever I have a project. Finally, I am thankful to God for giving me wisdom and strength to complete this work.

"He who has an ear, let him hear what the Spirit says to the churches" (Rev. 3:6).

Introduction

One crucial part of public worship—and often the longest part of each worship service—is the preaching of God's Word. Without a doubt, this is the most important part of public worship since it is God's primary means for saving sinners and sanctifying those who have already believed in Christ. Yet preaching is also the most difficult aspect of our worship service, not only for the pastor preaching behind the pulpit but also for the members listening in the pews.

During preaching, two things happen simultaneously. First, using the preacher as His instrument, God speaks to us; second, as God's Word is faithfully proclaimed, we are expected to listen. But good listening does not happen automatically! In fact, listening to a sermon that lasts thirty minutes or more can be a struggle for even the most devoted Christian. There are so many potential distractions—from physical weariness and our own personal thoughts and opinions to the things happening around us at any given moment. We have to be intentional if we are going to listen to sermons well. Yet, if we are truly honest with ourselves, many of us are not good listeners—let alone good sermon listeners.

One of the greatest problems in our churches today is poor listening. Too often we put the blame on our pastors when we are not sufficiently fed by the preaching of God's Word. We complain and tactlessly say, "Our pastor is not a good preacher." However, it is wrong for us to think that the blame for our dissatisfaction with public preaching should *always* fall on the pastor. Perhaps at times it does, since pastors are not perfect themselves. But if your pastor is genuinely preaching the full counsel of Scripture (as God has divinely commanded him to do) and seeking to do so effectively, then perhaps you should consider whether you are truly honoring God with the way you listen to sermons. All of us have surely struggled in this area and could stand to become better listeners, especially with regard to sermons. So, in humility, let us together seek to become more pleasing to God in the way that we listen to the preaching of His Word. In the following pages, I share ten biblical and practical ways that I believe we can and should follow with God's help.

Speak, O Lord, as we come to You
To receive the food of Your Holy Word.
Take Your truth, plant it deep in us;
Shape and fashion us in Your likeness,
That the light of Christ might be seen today
In our acts of love and our deeds of faith.
Speak, O Lord, and fulfill in us
All Your purposes for Your glory.

—Keith Getty, "Speak O Lord"

Chapter 1

Pray as You Listen

In 1 Samuel 3:10, Samuel spoke to God, saying, "Speak, for your servant hears." We can almost hear the eagerness in Samuel's voice as he pleads, "Lord, please speak to me, because I am listening to You. I am ready to hear what You want to say to me!" Like Samuel, we should communicate with God about our desire to hear from Him. We as listeners should participate in sermons by listening *prayerfully,* and we can do this in at least three ways.

First, pray *before* the sermon. Do you pray before the start of each worship service, asking God to speak to your heart? Do you thank the Lord for sending a preacher to teach God's Word to you, and do you ask the Lord to bless His servant? Are you intentional in asking God to make the sermon's message clear to you and to help you hear and receive the truth? Preparing our hearts for worship in this way—and asking God to remove any distractions that might prevent us from hearing from Him—can help us listen better as God's Word is proclaimed.

Second, we can also utter brief prayers *during* the sermon. Of course, it is important for us to be quiet and respectful during the message, listening to all that is preached from the pulpit and being careful not to distract others as God speaks to each of our hearts. But it is still appropriate to pray short, silent (or nearly silent) prayers to God as we hear Him clearly speaking to us through what is preached. This can be as simple as whispering a quick "Amen!" or "Thank you for this truth, God!" or as profound as asking God to forgive you for a sin of which you are convicted because of the sermon, or to help you live out a particular instruction being preached. By praying like this while we listen, we are in a sense seasoning the sermon with prayer, asking God to penetrate our hearts deeply with His powerful and life-changing Word. We must remember that the almighty God of heaven is actually speaking to us as His Word is preached, and we should be sure to receive His message in the appropriate way and in a spirit of genuine gratitude. Third, we should also remember to pray *after* each sermon, asking the Lord to help us remember and apply the truths we have just heard, so that we might grow not only in our listening but in our daily obedience to Him as well. God's Word exhorts us to become "doers of the word, and not hearers only" (James 1:22), and we can't possibly do this in our own abilities. We must remember to ask God to penetrate our hearts with His Word and to make us able to live what it teaches!

What is required of those that hear
the Word preached?

It is required of those that hear the word preached,
that they attend upon it with diligence (Prov. 8:34),
preparation (1 Peter 2:1–2; Luke 8:18), and prayer
(Ps. 119:18; Eph. 6:18–19); examine what they hear
by the Scriptures (Acts 17:11); receive the truth with
faith (Heb. 4:2), love (2 Thess. 2:10), meekness
(James 1:21), and readiness of mind (Acts 17:11), as
the Word of God (1 Thess. 2:13); meditate (Luke
9:44; Heb. 2:1), and confer of it (Luke 24:14; Deut.
6:6-7); hide it in their hearts (Prov. 2:1; Ps. 119:11),
and bring forth the fruit of it in their lives (Luke
8:15; James 1:25).

—Westminster Larger Catechism, Q&A 160

Chapter 2

Come Prepared

Because the preaching of God's Word is the most significant and challenging part of public worship, it requires mental, emotional, physical, and spiritual participation from not only the pastor but also the listeners.

For the pastor, preaching is an exhausting process. In fact, some think that preaching just one sermon is the equivalent of a full eight-hour work day. Thus, pastors who preach two sermons are working sixteen hours in one day. While others may not agree with this somewhat exaggerated statement, preaching two sermons in one day takes a ton of energy out of the preacher. Pastors also have to labor for hours *prior* to preaching in order to prepare the messages God has put on their hearts. In his article "How Much Time Do Pastors Spend Preparing a Sermon?" Thom S. Rainer concluded that "70% of pastors' sermon preparation time is the narrow range of 10 to 18 hours per sermon."[1] Obviously, good, biblical sermons don't write themselves. Pastors must devote many hours to praying, studying, and writing out their messages (and hopefully getting some rest!) before they stand before the congregation.

Because the preaching of God's Word is such a crucial part of God-honoring worship, the congregation must also come prepared to receive what God says to them. But this does not happen automatically. It requires some planning and special effort on our part, and we will benefit far more from each worship service—and each sermon—if we prepare ourselves in at least two ways.

First, we must prepare ourselves *spiritually*. Receiving the preached Word of God is challenging work; it requires alertness and active listening on our part. Yet it is also one of the most important things we do as growing Christians! Just as physical trainers teach athletes to stretch their muscles and warm-up prior to intense exercise, so we should take some time to "stretch our spiritual muscles" before we participate in public worship. This means we must

---

1. Thom S. Rainer, "How Much Time Do Pastors Spend Preparing a Sermon?," June 22, 2013, https://thomrainer.com/2013/06/how-much-time-do-pastors-spend-preparing-a-sermon/.

prepare our hearts and souls to receive biblical truth from God, truth that is sure to stretch us spiritually as we are clearly reminded of the awesomeness of God, the lostness of unbelievers, and even the lingering sinfulness of our own imperfect hearts. The glorious truths of Scripture should produce great joy in our hearts, but they are not always easy to receive, since they also call on us to confess sins and to change our lives in significant ways.

We should remember that prayer is the most important way for us to prepare ourselves spiritually for worship, as we ask God prior to each service to make our hearts receptive to whatever He wants to teach us. Another way to do this is to find out in advance what text is going to be preached (which is often posted in the church bulletin or on the church website) and to spend some time reading it and contemplating what it says, either the night before or the morning of the worship service. Take some time to pray over the specific passage of Scripture, asking God to help you understand it better as you hear it preached and to show you how to apply it to your own life. We can also prepare ourselves spiritually by singing hymns or listening to Christ-exalting music as we get ready for church.

Second, we must also prepare ourselves *physically* to worship God with our church family. It is easy for us to forget that our bodies are involved in worship too! We use our eyes to watch the pastor and read the Bible. We use our ears to hear the music and to listen to the preaching. We use our mouths to sing and to pray. Sometimes our legs are used for standing to sing or pray with our church family. Likewise, our mind is vital for all of these things and for contemplating the life-changing truths that are proclaimed to us from Scripture. Sometimes we try to distinguish the spiritual worship of God from anything that we do physically, but we can't do that. When we worship God, we do so physically.

This means that when our bodies are exhausted, it is hard to participate fully in worship. We're far less likely to benefit from the sermon if we are too tired to even listen to what is preached. We owe it to ourselves, to our church family, and certainly to God to be sufficiently rested prior to attending worship. Are we going to bed at a good time? Parents, are you making sure children get their sleep on Saturday night so that the entire family will have the physical energy to benefit from the church service? If you're blessed to attend a church that has two services on Sunday, are you faithful to attend both services as often as possible, and are you trying to rest before attending the evening service? Sometimes the most pious thing we can do on Sunday afternoon is take a nap so that we'll be physically prepared for the evening service. Whatever our particular schedule may look like, we should make every effort to limit our evening activities the night before we attend worship and to prepare ourselves physically as well as spiritually.

Open my ears, that I may hear
voices of truth you send so clear;
and while the message sounds in my ear,
everything false will disappear.
Silently now, on bended knee,
ready I wait your will to see;
open my ears, illumine me,
Spirit divine!

—Clara H. Scott, "Open My Eyes, That I May See"

Chapter 3

Excercise Patience

Sadly, our culture has helped make us all far less patient than we need to be. We live in a world full of impatient people who demand instant gratification from those who serve them. I'm afraid this self-centered way of thinking has now become tolerated, or even accepted, in our local churches. As a result, we seem to want everything *now*—from short worship songs to brief prayers to brief sermons. We have this same mentality virtually everywhere we go. We want fast service at restaurants and immediate access to information on our smartphones. We evaluate every invitation to do something with others by how much time it will take for us to participate. Even as we worship God, we want things to be fast and convenient; if they are not, we are quick to complain.

But listening as God speaks to us is not always fast or convenient. It is challenging work, and it often constitutes the longest part of our worship services.

Strangely, we seem to be able to watch a movie for hours or attend a long sporting event without complaining, but we want our worship services to end *precisely* on time so we can rush off to lunch and to the next thing on our schedule. If the preaching runs a bit too long by our standard, we are quick to complain to others in the church, and possibly even the pastor, that we feel that way. Don't we realize the damage we can cause by having such a critical attitude? We don't help anybody by trying to rush through our worship services, least of all ourselves. We need to learn to be patient!

We must remind ourselves that rich, deep, biblical sermons—sermons with substance that are able to feed our hungry souls, minister to our deepest hurts, and ultimately help us grow in Christlikeness—are rarely able to be delivered by a pastor in a mere fifteen minutes! According to Nehemiah 8:2–3, "So Ezra the priest brought the Law before the assembly, both men and women and all who could understand what they heard . . . from early morning until midday . . . And the ears of all the people were attentive to the Book of the Law." Just imagine! Ezra read God's Word to the people for *hours,* and they listened! In a similar way, we must remember to be patient as God's Word is faithfully expounded and to not allow other things to distract us from hearing what God wants to say to us. Nothing in all the world is more important to us than hearing from God, so we must be sure to make that the top priority of our lives. This requires us to be patient listeners when our pastors open God's Word and proclaim its truths to our hearts.

Wherefore when this Word of God is now preached
in the church by preachers lawfully called, we believe
that the very Word of God is proclaimed, and
received by the faithful;
and that neither any other Word of God is to be
invented nor is to be expected from heaven:
and that now the Word itself which is preached is to
be regarded, not the minister that preaches; for even
if he be evil and a sinner, nevertheless the Word of
God remains still true and good.

—The Second Helvetic Confession

Chapter 4

Revere the Lord

Ultimately, God Himself speaks to us through biblical sermons. Who is this God who speaks to us? He is the King of kings, the Lord of lords, the most high and holy God, and the almighty Creator of all things. He created us and rules over us, and we owe Him everything we have to offer. So, of course, we should remember to listen to Him reverently. It is true that we listen to our pastor preach week after week, but our pastor is merely the instrument through whom God has chosen to speak to us. Above and behind the words of any faithful preacher is the Lord God telling us how we should live. As John Calvin put it, "When the gospel is preached in the name of God, it is as if God himself spoke in person."[1]

In 1 Thessalonians 2:13, Paul says, "And we also thank God constantly for this, that when you received

---

1. Cited in John H. Leith, "Doctrine of the Proclamation of the Word," in Timothy Gorge, ed., *John Calvin and the Church: A Prism of Reform* (Louisville, KY: Westminster John Knox, 1990), 211.

the word of God, which you heard from us, you accepted it not as the word of men but as what it really is, the word of God, which is at work in you believers." Paul thanked God for the Thessalonians because when he preached the Word to them they recognized that it was not merely a word from Paul, but from God. This is how every Christian should receive the preaching of the Word: as coming from God Himself. When we remember this, it should motivate us to be reverent as we listen.

Ecclesiastes 5:1–2 exhorts all who approach the house of God for worship to "guard your steps," to "draw near to listen," and to "let your words be few." To put it another way, we should be reverent toward God when we are gathered for worship. We do this by being respectful and quiet when God is speaking to us through His Word. This does not simply mean we are not talking. It also means we must make every effort to keep our minds alert and focused on the message being preached. For if we allow ourselves to drift off to sleep or to think about other things during the sermon, it is as if we are saying to God, "Lord, what you have to say to me now really doesn't mean that much to me. I don't think it's very important."

Another way we seem to "interrupt" what God says to us during sermons is by refusing to accept all the Bible says as being absolutely true. Sometimes we silently argue with God as we listen to a message, trying to persuade Him that His words are not true or that they do not really apply to us. I know that whenever I try to instruct my children about things they do not agree with, their favorite response to me is, "But . . ." They will often say, "But Daddy . . . ," and I have to respond with, "No 'buts'—please just listen to me!" Yet we treat God this same way, saying, "But Lord, this can't be true" or "Lord, that command isn't really intended for me, is it?" Scripture reminds us that we must be "quick to hear, slow to speak" (James 1:19). We must listen to God! We have to allow Him to speak to us and remember that His words are perfect, true, and unchanging. Furthermore, He is good, loving, supremely wise, and—because He is all-knowing—He knows *exactly* what He is doing.

And he said to me, "Son of man, eat whatever
you find here.
Eat this scroll, and go, speak to the house of Israel."
So I opened my mouth, and he gave me
this scroll to eat.
And he said to me, "Son of man, feed your belly
with this scroll that I give you and fill
your stomach with it."
Then I ate it, and it was in my mouth
as sweet as honey.

—Ezekiel 3:1–3

Chapter 5

Be an Active Listener

When my children were young and first began to eat solid food, my wife or I had to help them eat. We would put the food in their mouths, but, of course, they had to actually chew and swallow the food. We could not do that for them. If we had eaten the food, then our children would not have been nourished by it. They were responsible for eating the food we gave to them.

A similar thing happens when God's Word is preached. A minister uses every possible means to explain what the Bible says, but listeners have the solemn responsibility to open their spiritual "mouths," chew the rich teaching of the Word, and swallow it completely into their very being. In fact, this is precisely the analogy that is used in Ezekiel 3:1–3, when God instructs the prophet Ezekiel, saying, "Feed your belly with this scroll that I give you." God's Word is spiritual food for our souls, and each of us is responsible for eating our own share of this food. It is not the preacher's job to eat our food for us—only to prepare the food and place it before us so we may eat it for ourselves. Yet, far too often, church members expect the preacher to spoon-feed them. However, receiving God's Word is our responsibility, not the pastor's. How often church members will complain, "I'm not being fed by the sermons!" If that's true, it is likely because we are failing to receive God's Word as we ought. We must be opening our mouths, chewing on the doctrines that are preached, and inwardly digesting and meditating on God's Holy Word. Our pastors can't do that for us.

Nehemiah 8:3 says, "And the ears of all the people were attentive to the Book of the Law." Consequently, the people were blessed by what they heard. They were strengthened by the Word because they listened attentively as it was proclaimed to them. It may sound gross, but after cows eat grass, they are able to regurgitate the grass and chew it again later so as to get the most nutrition out of it (this process is called rumination or, more commonly, "chewing the cud"). In some respect, that is what our reflection on biblical truth should look like: meditating on it over and over again so that we will be able to get the most profound and lasting benefit from our study of God's Word. As Augustine once declared, "The hearer of God's Word ought to be like those animals that chew the cud; he ought not only feed upon it, but to ruminate upon it."[1]

Bubble gum offers us a similar illustration of my point. I don't know about you, but when I chew bubble gum, typically I will not spit it out until I have gotten every bit of juice from it and there is no more sweet flavoring left. I want the full benefit of that piece of gum! Whether you chew gum or not, we should all be doing this with every sermon that we hear. Chew—ruminate—and meditate on God's Word until you have feasted sufficiently on what it says. Consider how the biblical message challenges your prior beliefs and actions, and allow what the Bible says to guide you in your next steps of obedience to God.

In the beloved hymn "Guide Me, O Thou Great Jehovah," we sing, "Bread of heaven, feed me till I want no more." This prayer should be ours too as we eagerly anticipate the spiritual food that God has in

---

1. Quoted in Isaac David Ellis Thomas, ed., *The Golden Treasury of Patristic Quotations* (Oklahoma City, OK: Hearthstone Publishing, 1996), 34.

store for us every time we assemble with His people for worship. In Psalm 81:10, God proclaims, "I am the LORD your God, who brought you up out of the land of Egypt. Open your mouth wide, and I will fill it." God promises that He will spiritually nourish us, but we have the responsibility to open our mouths so that we may receive from Him. If we want to leave every worship service satisfied and enriched by God's Word, then we must learn to actively listen to what is preached and "open our mouths" to receive the spiritual food being given to us.

Hear, O my people, while I admonish you!
O Israel, if you would but listen to me!
There shall be no strange god among you;
you shall not bow down to a foreign god.
I am the LORD YOUR GOD,
who brought you up out of the land of Egypt.
Open your mouth wide, and I will fill it.
"But my people did not listen to my voice;
Israel would not submit to me.
So I gave them over to their stubborn hearts,
to follow their own counsels.
Oh, that my people would listen to me,
that Israel would walk in my ways!
I would soon subdue their enemies
and turn my hand against their foes.
Those who hate the LORD WOULD CRINGE TOWARD HIM,
and their fate would last forever.
But he would feed you with the finest of the wheat,
and with honey from the rock I would satisfy you."

—Psalm 81:8–16

Chapter 6

Humble Yourself

In Psalm 81, God called for His people to be richly fed by His words, but then sadly concluded, "My people did not listen to my voice; Israel would not submit to me" (v. 11). How tragic that God's covenant people would not listen to Him! Rather than being humble and teachable before the God who created and ruled over them, they believed that they knew better and chose to act in rebellion against Him. Their disobedience offended and angered God, and they suffered terribly for it.

Sadly, we often behave the same way. We quickly fall into the wicked pattern of believing that our way is better than God's way, that *we* know better what we should do with our lives. What a terrible and presumptuous sin this is! We listen to sermons on familiar passages, thinking to ourselves, "Oh, sure, I've heard that message before" or "That's a good message for *those people,* but I don't really need to hear that myself." How easily the devil fills our hearts with pride if we allow him to do so!

No, my friends, we must remain humble and teachable, remembering that we can't live in a way that is pleasing to Him unless He guides us and enables us to do so and unless He forgives us of our many sins. We must never forget that we need God desperately. We depend on Him not only for our eternal salvation but even for the air we breathe, for the very next breath of air that fills our lungs and enables us to live a moment longer. We need God!

Therefore, we should regularly pray as Samuel did, "Speak, for your servant hears" (1 Sam. 3:10). Samuel regarded himself as God's servant and was therefore willing to listen to what He said and to obey His instructions. Do we have this same attitude ourselves? Do we recognize our total dependence on God and humble ourselves before Him so that we will be quick to hear and obey all that He says? As our Master and Lord speaks to us, are we listening in humility? We certainly should be!

When we gather together with our brothers and sisters in Christ for worship, we should do so in humility, recognizing that because of our sinfulness we are not worthy of the joys and blessings God provides. Yet He gives them to us because He loves us. The holy God of heaven calls us to come together with other believers in His presence, to hear Him speaking to us through the proclamation of His Word, and to grow deeper in our relationship with Him. We do not deserve such blessings! If we can remember just how blessed we are to know God in this way, and to be able to worship Him as we do, it will surely help us remain humble as we listen to the preaching of God's holy and unchanging Word.

The brothers immediately sent Paul and Silas
away by night to Berea,
and when they arrived they went into the
Jewish synagogue.
Now these Jews were more noble than those
in Thessalonica;
they received the word with all eagerness,
examining the Scriptures daily to see if these
things were so.

—Acts 17:10–11

Chapter 7

Discern What You Hear

According to Acts 17:11, the Berean Jews "were more noble than those in Thessalonica; they received the word with all eagerness, examining the Scriptures daily to see if these things were so." Preachers are not infallible. Though they are accountable to God for all they preach and make every effort to speak only God's truth, they can still make mistakes. For that reason, listeners must be careful to listen to sermons with discernment, carefully evaluating all that they hear according to Scripture to make sure they are truly being taught God's Word and not the mere opinions of man.

Our goal as we listen to sermons is not to be critical of everything we hear, seeking out every minor discrepancy or grammatical error. Of course, our enemy—the devil—would love to distract us by trying to make us into perfectionists who are so busy listening for insignificant mistakes that we completely miss the biblical truth being proclaimed. We should not be overly critical of the preacher or of his particular style of preaching. We should aim to listen closely to what is actually being taught and to hold up every claim made by the preacher to what the Bible plainly teaches.

If we are intent on being negative as we listen, we certainly should not expect to receive God's blessings. We must also remember that, while preachers are not perfect, we, as listeners, are not perfect either. We are both imperfect, and that is precisely the problem! Only God's Word is infallible, and only the gospel can overcome our sinfulness. That is exactly why we have such a desperate need for God's grace, mercy, and love! This will be our predicament until Jesus returns for His people, and that is why we all (pastors and laypeople alike) must approach worship—especially the proclamation of God's Word—with reverence and humility.

If we ever do believe that what we have heard a significant error in a sermon, we should make a point to go to our pastor personally—preferably away from other people—to discuss it. Practically, it is also best not to approach the pastor about this on Sunday (when he is already exhausted from sermon preparation and preaching) or Monday (which is often a day of rest and recuperation for pastors), but rather to try to meet with him during the next week sometime. As you wait to meet with him, you can make time to pray about the matter and plan out what you would like to say. It is always helpful to approach our pastors at the right time and with the right attitude when we want to discuss something we disagree with them about.

We should also seek to encourage our pastor as we do this (pastors already have plenty of things to discourage them in their labor), expressing our appreciation for the pastor's ministry before raising our particular concern to him. If you are unsure about the point that was made in the sermon, then perhaps your pastor can use Scripture to explain what he was saying more fully—and perhaps even to help you see that what he said was biblical. If the pastor was truly in error, though, then a good and faithful pastor should appreciate your attentiveness and discernment, and he will likely be grateful that you called the mistake to his attention. After all, pastors strive to be growing Christians too!

We are all called to listen with discernment to what is being taught to us, and this is especially crucial with regard to the things of God. We must always be sure that our beliefs and convictions are being governed not by personal opinions or speculation but by the unchanging truth of God's Word. As we continue to study the Bible and pray to the Holy Spirit to guide us into all truth, we will be better equipped to discern when God's Word is being faithfully proclaimed to us.

Beautiful words of Jesus,
Spoken so long ago,
Yet, as we sing them over,
Dearer to us they grow,
Calling the heavy laden,
Calling to hearts oppressed,
"Come unto Me, ye weary;
Come, I will give you rest."
Beautiful words of Jesus,
Tokens of endless rest,
When, by and by, we enter
Into His presence blest;
There shall we see His beauty,
Meet with Him face to face;
There shall we sing His glory,
Praising His matchless grace.

—Eliza E. Hewitt, "Beautiful Words of Jesus"

Chapter 8

Listen as an Act of Worship

If the sermon is the longest part of our worship service, then that means most of our time in worship is spent listening. Since God expects us to participate in our worship of Him, that means we can't be good worshipers of God unless we also become good listeners. Listening and worshiping go hand in hand: to listen to God's proclaimed Word is to worship the God of this Word. Let's also remember that we are worshiping God even as we listen!

Do you remember the biblical account of Mary and Martha in Luke 10:38–42? Consider again what this passage has to teach us:

> Now as they went on their way, Jesus
> entered a village. And a woman named
> Martha welcomed him into her house.
> And she had a sister called Mary, who sat
> at the Lord's feet and listened to his teach-
> ing. But Martha was distracted with much

serving. And she went up to him and said, "Lord, do you not care that my sister has left me to serve alone? Tell her then to help me." But the Lord answered her, "Martha, Martha, you are anxious and troubled about many things, but one thing is necessary. Mary has chosen the good portion, which will not be taken away from her."

Perhaps you don't realize this, but whenever you read or listen to God's Word, you are worshiping God, because reading or listening to His Word is a form of worship. That's why we must always approach God's Word—whether in our homes, in our churches, or anywhere else—with an attitude of *worship*. We are literally giving praise and glory to God by the way we make use of the Bible in our lives, and we should want Him to be pleased with how we worship Him! Do you listen to God's Word worshipfully?

"[Have] I become your enemy, because I tell you the truth?" When the surgeon comes to cure a corrupted wound; when he tears off the vile bandages which unskillful hands had wrapped around it; when he lays open the deepest recesses of your wound, and shows you all its venom and its virulence, do you call him cruel? May not his hands be all the time the hands of gentleness and love? Or, when a house is all on fire; when the flames are bursting out from every window; when some courageous man ventures to alarm the sleeping inmates, bursts through the barred door, tears aside the close-drawn curtains, and with eager hand shakes the sleeper, bids him awake and flee, "A moment longer and you may be lost," do you call him cruel; or do you say this messenger of mercy spoke too loud, too plain? Ah, no. . . . Why, then, brethren, will you blame the minister of Christ when he begins by convincing you of sin? Think you that the wound of sin is less venomous or deadly than a wound in the flesh? Think you the flames of hell are less hard to bear than the flames of earth? The very Spirit of love begins by convincing you of sin; and are we less the messengers of love because we too begin by convincing you of sin? Oh, then do not say that we have become your enemy because we tell you the truth.

—Robert Murray M'Cheyne

Chapter 9

Come with Expectations

If the almighty God is speaking to us through the preaching of His Word, we should certainly come to sermons with expectant hearts, trusting fully that God's Word will accomplish something wonderful in the lives of all who hear and receive it! In Isaiah 55:11 God tells us that "my word . . . shall not return to me empty, but it shall accomplish that which I purpose, and shall succeed in the thing for which I sent it." God does not waste His words on useless chatter! On the contrary, "every word that comes from the mouth of the Lord" (Deut. 8:3) is vital to our very existence, and we depend on His words for life, salvation, and the numerous other blessings that are available to us only through Him (Matt. 4:4).

We must come to worship with the great expectation that God will speak to us and bless us—that His words will accomplish something glorious in our hearts. Truly, no other words in all of creation compare to *His* words to us! We must listen to the preached Word of God with believing hearts, having faith that His words are true and that they have the power to transform lives for all eternity. We must come to Him, praying something like this: "Lord, I'm listening to You with great eagerness, knowing that You're going to feed me through the preaching of Your Word today, and that as a result I will be greatly blessed! As I worship You and hear from You, I have faith that You will 'feed me till I want no more'!"

Receiving God's Word is not always an easy process. In fact, sometimes it is a painful one. Why is that? Because, as Hebrews 4:12 teaches, "The word of God is living and active, sharper than any two-edged sword, piercing to the division of soul and of spirit, of joints and of marrow, and discerning the thoughts and intentions of the heart." When God's truth penetrates our hearts like a sharp sword, cutting out the sinful desires and separating them from us, it can frequently be an unpleasant experience. Even in these moments we should give thanks to God, recognizing that His rebukes and corrections are good for our souls and are ultimately helping us to become more like our Lord and Savior, Jesus Christ.

Do you really want to consider the Word of the
Gospel on a par with the word
or the talk of a peasant in an inn or a tavern?
Remember that God has said:
When the Word of Christ is preached,
I am in your mouth, and I pass with the Word
through your ears into your heart.
So, then, we have a sure sign and know that when
the Gospel is preached,
God is present and would have Himself found there.

—Martin Luther

Chapter 10

Receive the Word with Gratitude

As we read the Bible or hear its truths proclaimed in worship week after week, we are literally hearing from the merciful and gracious God who gave His only begotten Son, so that whosoever believes in His Son should not perish but have eternal life (John 3:16). How this thought should inspire us! Are we grateful to God as we hear this glorious truth of the gospel spoken to us from His Word? We certainly should be! In fact, the German Reformer Martin Luther was convinced that "when the Gospel is preached, God is present and would have Himself found there."[1] Imagine the great privilege we have: we not only hear God but also meet Him, for He is present with us whenever the gospel is proclaimed.

Ultimately, the preaching of God's Word points to Jesus Christ, since both the Old and New Testament

---

1. Ewald M. Plass, ed., *What Luther Says: A Practical In-Home Anthology for the Active Christian* (St. Louis: Concordia Publishing House, 1959), 1461.

find their fulfillment in Him, the Living Word of God. The message of Scripture is the message of Jesus Christ, who alone can save sinners and sanctify believers. How can we then take this lightly and not be emotionally stirred every time we hear God's words preached to us? Instead, we should say, "Lord, thank you for once again allowing me to hear from Your Holy Book and to meet Jesus there, who is the Bread of Life and the Living Water, the only one who can truly satisfy my soul. Thank you, God, for this joyous privilege and blessing! Thank you for the gospel! Thank you for Jesus, who is my all in all!"

Truly, we should come before God with grateful hearts, especially with regard to the precious gift of His Word and the salvation revealed in its pages! In the parable of the sower and the seeds (Matt. 13:1–23), the seed represents God's Word, and the four types of soil represent the different kinds of people who hear it. One kind of listener has a hard heart, one has a stony heart, and one has a heart like a path covered with thorns. But the fourth person has a good heart, receptive and eager to learn from God's Word, and is represented in the story by "good soil." Jesus ends the parable by saying, "He who has ears, let him hear" (v. 9). The Puritan preacher Thomas Watson once said, "It was by the ear, by our first parents listening to the serpent, that we lost paradise; and it is by the ear, by hearing of the Word, that we get to heaven. Hear, and your souls shall live.'"[2]

Our Lord and Savior exhorts us to listen to His words—and, in fact, to listen to all of Scripture—with great care and attention. In a similar way, Paul instructs young Timothy to "guard the good deposit entrusted" to him (2 Tim. 1:14), indicating that the gospel of salvation preserved within the pages of Scripture is a great treasure, which is to be guarded and cherished by all who love God. Do we treasure God's Word in this way? Are we thankful when it is preached and taught to us in a way that can feed our souls?

As we gather for worship and have the opportunity to hear Scripture preached in a way that honors God and exalts Christ, let us remember to give thanks to God for the honor of listening to it and for the blessings that will surely come to us as a result of receiving it!

---

2. Quoted in Isaac David Ellis Thomas, ed., *The Golden Treasury of Puritan Quotations* (Carlisle, PA: Banner of Truth, 1977), 221.

Dismiss us with Thy blessing Lord;
Help us to feed upon Thy word;
All that has been amiss, forgive,
And let Thy truth within us live.[3]

---

3. Joseph Hart, "Dismiss us with Thy blessing, Lord, Help us to feed upon Thy word," accessed August 4, 2018, https://hymnary.org/text/dismiss_us_with_thy_blessing_lord_help.

Conclusion

Needless to say, all the counsel offered in the preceding pages will be of very little benefit to you if you are not putting yourself under the clear and faithful preaching of the holy, unchanging, eternally edifying Word of God on a regular basis! God, in His infinite wisdom, has ordained for all who follow Him to be a part of the eternal family of God and therefore to become active members of a local church where part of this family gathers regularly for worship, prayer, and ministry.

Many passages of Scripture express the importance of faithfully attending church, including Hebrews 10:24–25, which calls us to "consider how to stir up one another to love and good works, not neglecting to meet together, as is the habit of some, but encouraging one another, and all the more as you see the Day drawing near." We are encouraging Christian growth in both ourselves and others by simply attending worship on a regular basis! Furthermore, if we aren't being fed a rich diet of biblical truth alongside our brothers and sisters in Christ, we will surely become spiritually malnourished! Throughout its pages, the Bible describes itself as food and drink for our souls, light for the paths we travel, the very words of God to us, and the revelation of all we need to know about God. So how could we neglect to listen to the rich truths of God's Word—by reading it, studying it, praying over it, and hearing it faithfully preached by people whom God has gifted to do so—as often as we possibly can?

Therefore, my hope, prayer, and closing exhortation for all who read this book (and for myself!) is that all of us will be faithful to listen to God's Word—and to the preaching of it—as often as we are able to do so. Christians who aren't pastors must be sure to seek out and become active members of churches where God's Word is clearly, faithfully, and boldly proclaimed in all its fullness. Those whom God has called to preach must endeavor to proclaim God's Word faithfully and accurately, with soberness and humility, recognizing that they too should seek out opportunities to hear God's Word preached by others (if not in person, then certainly by reading published sermons or listening to recordings from other faithful pastors). Like all believers, they must strive to submit themselves to all that God's Word says to us.

As each of us continues to place ourselves under the regular, faithful preaching of God's Word, the delight and blessing we find in listening to God speak to us will surely continue to grow, and we will increasingly become not only better *hearers* but also better *doers* of God's Word! May God plant a love for His Word deeply into each of our hearts and help us to grow in our zeal for listening to it!

Appendix 1

Five Kinds of Hearers of God's Word[1]

"But be doers of the word, and not hearers only, deceiving yourselves. For if anyone is a hearer of the word and not a doer, he is like a man who looks intently at his natural face in a mirror. For he looks at himself and goes away and at once forgets what he was like. But the one who looks into the perfect law, the law of liberty, and perseveres, being no hearer who forgets but a doer who acts, he will be blessed in his doing." (James 1:22–25)

1. **Mr. Blind.** He is blind and thus unable to see the spots on his face in a mirror. Others see his flaws, but he cannot see them because of his spiritual blindness. He is so blind that he calls evil good and good evil. He is not bothered by living in sin.

2. **Mr. Afraid.** He knows he has some spots on his face but is afraid to look at them in a mirror. He

---

1. A version of this appendix appeared previously in *The Outlook* 65, no. 2 (2015): 11. Used by permission.

is like a person who knows he has a health problem but is afraid to see a doctor. Mr. Afraid cannot accept reality. He tries to avoid the truth and does not want to be confronted by God's Word.

3. **Mr. Self-Righteous.** He looks at his face in a mirror and notices some spots, but he does not do anything about his face. He deceives himself by thinking he is good when in fact he is bad. He thinks he is good enough to go to heaven. When exhorted to change his wicked behavior, he reasons, "I don't need to change. My neighbor does, but not me."

4. **Mr. Pessimistic.** He looks at his face in a mirror and sees his blemishes but thinks they are too great to be washed. Mr. Pessimistic knows he is a sinner but thinks his sins are too great to be forgiven. He dwells on his misery. He despairs, saying, "I am too sinful to be saved." Mr. Pessimistic needs to learn from the Scottish minister Robert Murray M'Cheyne, who beautifully states, "For every look at self, take ten looks at Christ."

5. **Mr. Wise.** He looks at his face and sees his spots in a mirror and cleanses his face—that is, when he notices his sins by looking at God's Word, he comes to God for forgiveness in Christ. He prays with the tax collector, "God, be merciful to me, a sinner!" James says this kind of person will be blessed (1:25).

Which kind of hearer are you?

Appendix 2

How to Criticize a Preacher[1]

So you've heard a sermon and you're not happy. You feel the preacher got it badly wrong in either his interpretation, his words, his manner, his length, his whatever.

What now?

Well, I'm not going to tell you exactly what words to use. I'm simply going to give you ten questions to ask that I hope will produce the right words and the right way to say them should you ever have to offer criticism to a preacher.

1. **Have I understood him correctly?** Give the preacher the benefit of the doubt. Ask yourself, "Am I putting the worst possible spin on this?" Perhaps check with your husband or wife, "Did I hear this correctly . . . ?"

1. This appendix is by David P. Murray. It is available from his blog, HeadHeartHand: http://headhearthand.org/blog/.

2. **Have I given this enough time?** It's rarely wise or helpful to immediately react to what is preached. Your passions will be high, but so will the preacher's. Not a good recipe.

3. **Have I prayed about this?** Have you taken time to ask, "Lord show me if I'm right here. Show me if this is important enough to take further. Help me to see if this is primary or a secondary matter"?

4. **Is this just personal preference or biblical principle?** We all have our favorite truths and our favorite preaching styles. Is this about Bible doctrines and biblical practice, or just my tradition or preference?

5. **Have I thought about the best time and way to communicate?** Neither Sunday or Monday are good days to approach a pastor about problems with his preaching. On Sunday, his adrenaline is still pumping. On Monday, he's flat as a pancake. Best not do this in public in front of others but in private. Do it in a calm, gentle, and loving manner. As I've learned, do it personally

rather than in writing or by email.

6. **Am I doing this out of the right motive?** Is my love and respect obvious? If it is constructive, designed to serve the pastor, then criticism can be incredibly helpful.

7. **Am I focused or just spraying pellets?** Never say, "And while we're at it, that sermon last year . . . and here's another thing . . ."

8. **Have I considered the possibility I may be one of many others doing the same?** You may be the straw that breaks the preacher's back.

9. **Am I prepared to listen to his explanation and concede I was wrong?** Are you genuinely open to be corrected yourself?

10. **Is it in the context of previously expressed appreciation?** It's so much easier to listen to criticism when you know the person has your good at heart and wants you to thrive and prosper. The repeated critic can be much more easily ignored or dismissed.

Fifteen Pointers for Preachers[1]

1. **Preach sound doctrine.** Don't reserve Bible doctrines such as justification and sanctification for your Sunday school. Preach these doctrines during your worship service.

2. **Preach with discrimination.** Address both believers and unbelievers in your preaching. Don't assume that everyone in your congregation is saved, but neither assume that no one is saved.

3. **Preach with an application.** Apply your text to your listeners. With the use of practical illustrations, help them apply your message to their daily lives. A sermon without an application is like a lecture. You are preaching, not lecturing.

4. **Preach clearly.** Organize your thoughts. Avoid difficult words. Consider the children in your congregation. If you have to employ a big word (e.g., justification), explain it using simple words.

---

1. A version of this appendix originally appeared in *Puritan Reformed Journal* 6, no. 2 (2014): 284–86. Used by permission.

5. **Preach the gospel.** Yes, preach against sin, but don't stop there. Preach about salvation, too. If you preach the law without the gospel, you will make your congregation despair. Further, don't think that the gospel is only for unbelievers. Believers need it for their sanctification as well.

6. **Preach with power.** Preach with the unction of the Holy Spirit, as the apostle Paul did: "My speech and my message were not in plausible words of wisdom, but in demonstration of the Spirit and of power, so that your faith might not rest in the wisdom of men but in the power of God" (1 Cor. 2:4–5).

7. **Preach prayerfully.** Pray before, during, and after you preach. Humbly acknowledge that without God's help, you can do nothing. Realize that God alone can change the hearts of your listeners.

8. **Preach with expectations.** Remember that nothing is impossible with God. Expect greatly that He will do wondrous things—saving sinners and sanctifying saints. Be confident that His Word will not return to Him void. He can even use your worst sermon to accomplish His wonderful plan.

9. **Preach persuasively.** Show that what you proclaim is God's Word. Announce, "Thus says

the LORD." Also, don't be afraid to declare God's truths, even if by doing so some of your hearers might be offended. You are to please God, not people.

10. **Preach passionately.** Love not only preaching but also the people to whom you preach. When you love your congregation, you will feed them with spiritually nutritious food.

11. **Preach faithfully.** Be faithful to your announced text(s). Don't just read your text and leave it. Use it. Expound it. Preach from it.

12. **Preach seriously.** The very Word that you preach is sacred. The God who has called you to preach is holy. Your message is a matter of life and death, heaven and hell. Thus, jokes have no place in the pulpit. Preachers are not called to be entertainers.

13. **Preach with Christ at the center.** Learn from Paul who says, "I . . . did not come proclaiming to you the testimony of God with lofty speech or wisdom. For I decided to know nothing among you except Jesus Christ and him crucified" (1 Cor. 2:1–2). In the words of the Puritan preacher William Perkins (1558–1602), "Preach one Christ, by Christ, to the praise of Christ."

14. **Preach what you live.** Live what you preach. Demonstrate holiness, not hypocrisy. Acknowledge with Robert Murray M'Cheyne (1813–1843), "My people's greatest need is my personal holiness."

15. **Preach to the glory of God alone.** Your ultimate goal in preaching is to glorify God. Never attempt to take that glory that belongs to God alone. Sing with Fanny J. Crosby (1820–1915), "To God be the glory, great things He has done."

Oh, Lord, help me to preach!

Appendix 4

Two Extremes to Avoid in Preaching[1]

Extreme # 1: Preaching as if *everyone* in the congregation is saved.

Years ago I received an email from a member of a certain congregation. This person, whom I did not know personally at the time I received the email, was wondering why their pastor preached as if everyone in their church was saved. And because their pastor viewed everyone in the pews as regenerate, he did not see the need to call his congregation to self-examination. In other words, since in this preacher's mind everyone in his local church was saved, he only delivered messages that addressed the believers. In his sermons, there was no direct call for the unbelievers to repent of their sins and believe in the Lord Jesus Christ for their salvation.

---

1. A version of this appendix appeared previously in *The Outlook* 68, no. 4 (2018): 20–21. Used by permission.

I have some problems with this kind of preaching. First of all, a preacher who assumes that everyone in the congregation is saved has an idealistic view of a local church. The truth is, there is no absolutely pure local church composed of only true believers. A visible church will always have both goats and sheep—a sad and painful reality for ministers. And both the goats and the sheep need the gospel: the goats for their salvation, the sheep for their sanctification. Until Christ returns, the congregations that we serve will remain impure (Matt. 25:31–46). Therefore, a pastor should keep in mind that as he proclaims God's Word, there might be at least one unbeliever present during the preaching. Furthermore, a pastor who does not see the need to call his congregation to self-examination on the basis of his assumption that everyone is saved might create a false sense of assurance of salvation among the unbelievers.

Moreover, self-examination is not only for unbelievers but also for believers. Writing to the Corinthian church, Paul says, "Examine yourselves, to see whether you are in the faith. Test yourselves. Or do you not realize this about yourselves, that Jesus Christ is in you?—unless indeed you fail to meet the test!" (2 Cor. 13:5). Here

Paul is particularly addressing his fellow believers. The truth that self-examination is also for believers appears in our "Liturgical Form for the Celebration of the Lord's Supper," in which we are exhorted to examine ourselves before partaking of the Lord's Supper: "That we may now celebrate the supper of the Lord to our comfort, it is necessary, before all things, rightly to examine ourselves. . . . Let every one examine his heart whether he also believes this sure promise of God that all his sins are forgiven him only for the sake of the passion and death of Jesus Christ, and that the complete righteousness of Christ is imputed and freely given him as his own—yea, so completely as if he himself, in his own person, had satisfied for all his sins and fulfilled all righteousness."[2]

Here's my point: Believers in Christ also need to examine whether they themselves truly believe in Jesus or not. And the purpose of this examination is not to make them doubt but to drive them even closer to Christ.

---

2. See "Liturgical Form for the Celebration of the Lord's Supper," in *Psalter Hymnal* (Grand Rapids: Board of Publications of the Christian Reformed Church, 1976), 143.

Extreme # 2: Preaching as if *no one* in the congregation is saved.

Some pastors preach as if *no one* in their congregations is saved (they do the exact opposite of what the previous pastors do). Or, more accurately, these pastors assume that most of their hearers are unsaved and that only a minority among their audience who are truly saved. As a result, many members of their congregations—who are genuine believers—suffer severely from a lack of assurance of salvation. Imagine sitting under such preaching. Eventually, you (as a believer) will begin to question the genuineness of your salvation in an unhealthy way, and then fall into despair.

Several years ago I met an old man who sat under this kind of preaching. He was in his nineties and had been a member of this congregation for over fifty years. Yet sadly he did not know whether he was saved or not. This man went to church twice every Sunday for many years and served as an elder several times, but he had no assurance of salvation. Ironically, for this man the more you doubt the more pious you become. Thus, in his mind, doubt is a form of virtue.

Well, such thinking contradicts what Peter says: "Therefore, brothers, be all the more diligent to confirm your calling and election" (2 Peter 1:10). Here Peter is commanding his fellow believers to make sure of their calling and election. And yes, it is possible for Christians to experience and enjoy assurance of salvation. As the Canons of Dort says, "Of this preservation of the elect to salvation, and of their perseverance in the faith, true believers for themselves may and do obtain assurance according to the measure of their faith." Charles Spurgeon once observed, "Many a believer lives in the cottage of doubt when he might live in the mansion of faith."

Pastors who commit the second extreme in preaching should realize the damage they do to their members—namely, they foster a spirit of doubt and despair among those who are sincerely saved.

Conclusion

How can we then avoid these two extremes in preaching? There are many ways, but for the sake of time, let me just give you one—that is, *be faithful to your text*. Don't just read your text and leave it. Use it. Expound it. Preach from it. And don't force your text to say something that it does not say. As a preacher, you are to tell your congregation what your text says.

Suppose your text is Romans 8:28–29: "And we know that for those who love God all things work together for good, for those who are called according to his purpose. For those whom he foreknew he also predestined to be conformed to the image of his Son." Obviously this text is for believers, so use this text to address them in your sermon. However, in that same sermon (even just in a few words), you can also warn the wicked by saying that all things are not working together for their eternal good, because the glorious promise found in this passage is only for those who love God.

Now, if your text is Revelation 21:8, then address the unbelievers in your sermon: "But as for the cowardly, the faithless, the detestable, as for murderers, the sexually immoral, sorcerers, idolaters, and all liars, their portion will be in the lake that burns with fire and sulfur, which is the second death." With this passage, don't hesitate to challenge the unbelievers to repent and believe in Jesus Christ. And as you do so, in passing you can comfort and assure your fellow believers that their portion will not be in the lake of fire but in the new heaven and new earth.

Of course, you can also preach from a passage that *naturally* addresses both the believers and the unbelievers. Some of the parables of Jesus do this (e.g., wise and foolish builders [Matt. 7:24–27]; wise and foolish virgins [Matt. 25:1–13]; and sheep and goats [Matt. 25:31–46]). These passages allow the pastor to address both the righteous and the wicked in his sermon in a natural and balanced way.

Nevertheless, let me issue a word of caution here for those who listen to a sermon: you cannot expect your pastor to deliver a well-balanced sermon that deals equally with the godly and the ungodly. Depending on the text, sometimes the message can be geared more toward the believers and sometimes more toward the unbelievers. Therefore, if you want to evaluate your pastor, do so based on his faithfulness to his text. The question should not be whether he addressed the unbelievers or not in his message, or whether he addressed the believers or not. No! Instead, did he faithfully preach and apply his text to his congregation?

Appendix 5:

Respect the Time Your Pastor Needs for Prayer and Sermon Preparation

One Calvinist Baptist minister who came out of eighteenth-century evangelicalism was Samuel Pearce (1766–1799), who, in the words of Susan Huntington (1791–1823), was "pre-eminently a holy man."[1] Pearce was the pastor of Cannon Street Baptist Church in Birmingham, England, where he served diligently and faithfully from 1790 until his death in 1799. With God's blessing, the Birmingham church grew spiritually and numerically under his preaching; more than three hundred souls were converted and became members of his congregation. Pearce "regularly preached three times on the Lord's Day and usually in neighboring villages two or three times during the week."[2] During his ministry, he established a Sunday

---

1. Cited in *The Piety of Samuel and Sarah Pearce: Joy Unspeakable and Full of Glory,* ed. and intro. by Michael A. G. Haykin (Kitchener, ON: Joshua Press, 2012), xix.
2. *The Piety of Samuel and Sarah Pearce,* 8.

school, benevolent society to assist the poor, and a sick society to care for the afflicted.

When William Belsher was ordained pastor in the Baptist congregation in Worcester, Worcestershire, it was Pearce who gave the ordination sermon. In this sermon, which was based on Ephesians 4:11, Pearce urged lovingly the church members to respect and protect their pastor's time for prayer and study of God's Word—the pastor's two primary ministries listed in Acts 6:4, "But we will devote ourselves to prayer and to the ministry of the word."

Pearce said in that sermon,

> I want to convince you that, for your own sakes, you should promote a studious habit in your minister; allow him every inch of time he wants; neither call upon him, nor expect him to call upon you for no better purpose than to gossip; especially let his *mornings* and his *Saturdays* be sacred—it is little short of cruelty to interrupt him then. As you love him, so, no doubt, you will feel a pleasure in his company; but let him choose his own times for seeing you; and do not accuse him of criminal negli-

gence, if his visits are less frequent than you expect. Perhaps at the very moment of your disappointment, he was studying something against the Lord's Day for your case—perhaps at the moment you are censuring him for his neglect, he is wrestling with God for you in his closet.[3]

Commenting on Pearce's message, church historian Michael Haykin (to whom I am indebted for my own study of Pearce) writes, "Here Pearce surely speaks from personal experience of the tension that pastors in the Protestant tradition have repeatedly faced: the need to devote substantial time to sermon-preparation and prayer while also caring for the souls of those in their churches."[4]

Pastors of large congregations especially struggle with this tension. What is striking, though, in Pearce's admonition is the fact that the church members are to respect their pastor's personal prayer and sermon preparation time *for their own sake.* Now, if you are a church member, you might say, "How can this be

---

3. John Ryland, Jr. and Samuel Pearce, *The Duty of Ministers to be Nursing Fathers to the Church; and the Duty of Churches To Regard Ministers as the Gift of Christ* (London, 1796), 51–52. Italics original. I owe this quote to Haykin.
4. *The Piety of Samuel and Sarah Pearce,* 12.

for my own sake?" Well, imagine having a pastor who does not have sufficient time to intercede regularly for you. Imagine a pastor who does not have enough time to study for his sermons. You obviously want to hear good sermons from your pastor; but good sermons do not write themselves. Your pastor must devote many hours to praying, studying, and writing his messages (and hopefully getting some rest!) before he stands behind the pulpit. In his article "How Much Time Do Pastors Spend Preparing a Sermon?" Thom Rainer concludes, "70% of pastors' sermon preparation time is the narrow range of 10 to 18 hours per sermon."[5]

Let's just say your pastor needs fifteen hours to prepare for one sermon. If he preaches twice, then thirty hours of his time is spent just for sermon preparation. He still has other duties such as meetings to attend, visits to make, members to counsel, emails to reply to, phone calls to make, Sunday school or catechism lessons to prepare, a family to take care of, and other unexpected responsibilities such as a funeral. If you don't respect your pastor's time for sermon preparation, the entire congregation will suffer eventually by having

5. "How Much Time Do Pastors Spend Preparing a Sermon?," https://thomrainer.com/2013/06/how-much-time-do-pastors-spend-preparing-a-sermon/.

a half-cooked sermon, which can result in spiritual malnourishment among the members.

If you are an elder in your church, you have the responsibility to make sure your pastor is getting enough time for personal prayer and study of God's Word. Remember, your pastor is to devote himself "to prayer and to the ministry of the word." Of course, it does not mean that the pastor should not engage in other ministries. As God enables him, he should also, for instance, visit his members, especially the needy ones. However, some elders have unrealistic expectations from their pastor, asking their pastor to do more than he is able. As a result, their pastor burns out and becomes ineffective in the ministry, which in turn affects the entire life of the church.

Elders should regularly ask their pastor, "Are you getting enough rest? Are you still able to exercise? Are you still able to fulfill your holy duty as a husband and father? How is your prayer life? Are you still able to pray for us on a regular basis, not just on Sunday or during prayer meeting? Are you getting enough time for sermon preparation?" A pastor should honestly answer these questions, so that his elders can properly help him for the sake of their congregation.

About the Author

Born and reared in the Philippines, **Brian G. Najapfour** has been a minister of God since 2001. Called to the gospel ministry at the young age of sixteen, he began his theological education in 1997 at the Center for Biblical Studies Institute and Seminary in the Philippines. There, with God's help, he earned his Bachelor of Theology (B.Th.) degree in 2001, followed by his Master in Biblical Studies (M.B.S.) degree in 2004. From 2001 until his coming to the U.S. in 2006, he served as a pastor in the Philippines. With a desire to further his education, however, he arrived in Grand Rapids, Michigan, in 2006, where he enrolled in Puritan Reformed Theological Seminary. There, he studied for his Master of Theology (Th.M.) degree, which he completed by God's grace in 2009.

From 2012 to 2017 he pastored Dutton United Reformed Church, Caledonia, Michigan. He is currently working full-time on a PhD in Biblical

Spirituality under the supervision of Dr. Michael Haykin at The Southern Baptist Theological Seminary, Louisville, Kentucky.

He and his wife, Sarah, have four children, Anna, James, Abigail, and Grace. For more information about him, visit his website: biblicalspiritualitypress.org.

Other Books by the Author

Taking Hold of God: Reformed and Puritan Perspectives on Prayer (co-editor)

The Very Heart of Prayer: Reclaiming John Bunyan's Spirituality

Jonathan Edwards: His Doctrine of & Devotion to Prayer

Child Dedication: Considered Historically, Theologically, and Pastorally

The Gospel-Driven Tongue: Lessons from James on Godly Conversation

Amazing Grace, first part of the series called "Stories behind Favorite Hymns for Ages 3 to 6" (co-author)

The Collected Prayers of John Knox (editor)

Note to the Reader

The publisher invites you to respond to us about this book by writing to Reformed Fellowship, Inc., at *president@reformedfellowship.net*

Founded in 1951, Reformed Fellowship, Inc., is a religious and strictly nonprofit organization composed of a group of Christian believers who hold to the biblical Reformed faith. Our purpose is to advocate and propagate this faith, to nurture those who seek to live in obedience to it, to give sharpened expression to it, to stimulate the doctrinal sensitivities of those who profess it, to promote the spiritual welfare and purity of the Reformed churches, and to encourage Christian action.

Members of Reformed Fellowship express their adherence to the Calvinistic creeds as formulated in the Belgic Confession, the Heidelberg Catechism, the Canons of Dort, and the Westminster Confession and Catechisms.

To fulfill our mission, we publish a bimonthly journal, *The Outlook*, and we publish books and Bible study guides. Our website is *www.reformedfellowship.net*.

MORE BIBLE STUDY MATERIALS AVAILABLE FROM REFORMED FELLOWSHIP!

Purchase online at www.reformedfellowship.net
or email: sales@reformedfellowship.net

Amos Bible Studies
Rev. Henry Vander Kam
Paperback, 96 pages

Daniel Bible Studies
Rev. John Piersma
Paperback, 80 pages

Esther
The God Who Is Silent Is Still Sovereign
Norman De Jong
Paperback, 88 pages

Genesis 1-11 Bible Studies
Rev. Mark Vander Hart
Paperback, 186 pages

The Gospel-Driven Tongue:
Lessons from James on Godly Conversation
Rev. Brian G. Najapfour
Paperback, 72 pages

Gospel Power Magnified through Human Weakness
(2 Corinthians)
Dr. Nelson Kloosterman
Paperback, 101 pages

Jacob Bible Studies
Rev. Mark Vander Hart
Paperback, 156 pages

Joseph & Judah Bible Studies
Rev. Mark Vander Hart
Paperback, 80 pages

Letter to the Ephesians
Rev. Henry Vander Kam
Paperback, 132 pages

Meeting Jesus at the Feast:
Israel's Festivals and the Gospel
Dr. John R. Sittema
Paperback, 160 pages

1 Peter Bible Studies
Rev. Henry Vander Kam
Paperback, 165 pages

Ruth Bible Studies
Dr. L. Charles Jackson
Paperback, 176 pages

1 & 2 Thessalonians Bible Studies
Rev. Henry Vander Kam
Paperback, 136 pages

1 Timothy Bible Studies
Rev. Henry Vander Kam
Paperback, 112 pages

2 Timothy & Titus Bible Studies
Rev. Henry Vander Kam
Paperback, 100 pages

The Future of Everything: Essential Truths About the End Times
Rev. William Boekestein
Paperback, 160 pages

The Law of the Lord as Our Delight (Deuteronomy)
Dr. Nelson Kloosterman
Paperback, 100 pages

The Parables of Our Lord
Rev. Henry Vander Kam
Paperback, 66 pages

Bible Studies on Mark
Rev. William Boekestein
Paperback, 212 pages

LIFE IN CHRIST CATECHISM SERIES:

Not My Own
by Glenda Mathes
Intermediate (Grades 5 and 6)
Spiral bound, 168 pages

God's Unfolding Promise
by Laurie Vanden Heuvel
Intermediate (Grades 5 and 6)
Spiral bound, 216 pages

Christ's Living Church
by Rev. Ronald Scheuers
Middle School (Grades 7 and 8)
Spiral bound, 232 pages

Faith of Our Fathers
by Revs. Bradd L. Nymeyer and Al Bezuyen
Middle School (Grades 7 and 8)
Spiral bound, 200 pages

The Price of Possession 1
by Dr. Warren H. Lammers
High School (Grades 9 through 12)
Spiral bound, 232 pages

The Price of Possession 2
by Dr. Warren H. Lammers
High School (Grades 9 through 12)
Spiral bound, 232 pages

The Doctrines of Grace
by Revs. John A. Bouwers and Ronald L. Scheuers
High School (Grades 9 through 12)
Spiral bound, 232 pages

Facing Faith's Challenges
by Rev. Andrew A. Cammenga
High School (Grades 9 through 12)
Spiral bound, 208 pages

**Please visit:
www.reformedfellowship.net
for a full listing of our books!**